Spiritual Insights of T. W. Willingham

Book 6

Crumbs That Challenge the Saints

Part 1

Crumbs That Challenge the Saints

Part 1

Beacon Hill Press of Kansas City
Kansas City, Missouri

ISBN: 083-411-1667

Printed in the
United States of America

Cover design: Crandall Vail

Permission to quote from *The Living Bible* (TLB), © 1971 by Tyndale House
Publishers, Wheaton, Ill., is acknowledged with appreciation.

10   9   8   7   6   5   4   3   2   1

Contents

Foreword

Dr. T. W. Willingham is almost a legend in the Church of the Nazarene. He has served as pastor, district superintendent, college president, and executive at the world headquarters of the church.

Somewhat like Bernard Baruch he has been a close advisor to general superintendents and fledgling executive directors over the years. His business acumen and practical judgment have been sought after by all of us.

His greatest impact, however, has been in the spiritual realm. I and literally thousands have been stimulated by his insight into the Scriptures. Take these "crumbs," which I consider the most prophetic (prophetlike) pieces that have ever come from our presses, and revel in them.

—M. A. (Bud) Lunn

A Note of Thanks

First, I desire to thank my God for giving me time, strength, and guidance during the past 40 years as I have worked on the 16 books that I have had published.

In 1970, the Lord gave me a five-page directive concerning my writings in which He said, "I have given you two helpers . . . and it is My desire that they help you, and if they abide near Me they will feel the same way."

These two God-given workers—Clara Rogers and Kathy Butts—have been dependable and efficient and, more important, have felt that in so laboring they have been serving the Master and His kingdom.

Clara has corrected nearly all my handwritten articles, as well as typing many. Kathy has typed much, organized material, and by research and study, has made many valuable contributions. I thank God for both of them; without such help my work could not have been done.

If these messages prove to be of spiritual help to you, just give all the praise to our Heavenly Father.

—T. W. WILLINGHAM

Lest They Should Be Put Out

(John 12:42)

Before discussing the truth under consideration, we should have its context before us. It reads:

"Nevertheless among the chief rulers also many believed on him; but because of the Pharisees they did not confess him, lest they should be put out of the synagogue: for they loved the praise of men more than the praise of God" (John 12:42-43).

Herein we have illustrated a widespread weakness of the human race, and a prolific cause for spiritual defeat. The miraculous work of Jesus, especially the raising of Lazarus, had turned multitudes to Him, insomuch that many of the chief rulers believed on Him. Then came the test. Would they be willing to make known their secret belief and confess Him as Lord? To do this was to bring down upon themselves the wrath of the Pharisees and ejection from the synagogue.

The public announcement was a requirement: "For with the heart man believeth unto righteousness; and with the mouth confession is made unto salvation" (Rom. 10:10).

The Master's promise was: "Whosoever therefore shall confess me before men, him will I confess also before my Father which is in heaven. But whosoever shall deny me before men, him will I also deny before my Father which is in heaven" (Matt. 10:32-33).

The public confession was necessary but costly, "for the Jews had agreed already, that if any man did confess that he was Christ, he should be put out of the synagogue" (John 9:22). A place in the synagogue was the highest honor that man could bestow; hence these chief rulers were face-to-face with an issue of eternal consequences. They decided the matter according to their love. "They loved the praise of men more than the praise of God"—hence, they turned Christ down.

This brings us to the heart of man's greatest problem. Jesus focused attention on it when He said, "Thou shalt love the Lord thy God with all thy heart." He again reminded His followers that they must put Him above all others.

To put the praise of men above the praise of God is to elevate the creature above the Creator, and that is not allowable. By this common practice, God is crowded out of the lives of many to their eternal loss.

There are many reasons why men thus act. One is the unwillingness to suffer by departing from the herd. Man is by nature and by birth attached to the herd, and he becomes a "speckled bird" when he decides to pursue the narrow Way. It is easier to follow the throng than to leave it, and man is inclined to take the easier route.

Another reason why men hesitate to fully accept Christ is because they love the visible more than the invisible. They hold to what they can see and feel—the things that the senses embrace and not the things that are reached only by faith. Sight dominates the horizon, while faith dies of disuse. The visible is near, the invisible far away, so the one at hand is chosen.

Another prominent factor is man's desire to be accepted. He dislikes rejection, and since the masses are going the broad way, to go the narrow Way is to be set aside by others.

A more deceptive factor is the delusiveness of human praise. It is overvalued. One may do a lot of living before he

10

realizes just how transitory human praise is. Flattery is one of Satan's prized weapons in deception. Praise sounds so attractive, and yet it can be so quickly turned into criticism. It often lives but for a few moments, and never beyond time. Like the mist of the morning, it is soon passing.

Then, too, to obtain the praise of God there are changes that must be made in one's life. The whole pattern of living must be altered. A new alignment must be made, and change does not always appeal to one. It is easier to maintain the status quo.

Perhaps the greatest problem involved here is man's unwillingness to fully yield himself to the Master that he might obtain His praise. The praise of men is cheap; the praise of the Master is valuable, and valuables come high. The surrender of self is involved, and self is loathe to yield.

So we have in these chief rulers a group of typical people of all ages—men who are set on the temporal to the neglect of the eternal; in love with that which is physically enjoyable, rather than that which is spiritually profitable; those who live by sight and not by faith.

The whole picture is unclear until one draws the curtain aside and views the last showing, for the scene is not ended at the grave. No final appraisal can be made without looking beyond the boundaries of this earthly life. When thus viewed, what do we see?

To have the praise of God is to live with Him eternally. Those who settle for the earthly must be forever excluded from the heavenly. It is when thus viewed that the tragedy of choosing the praise of men appears.

What value will man's encomiums have when passing time has faded into endless eternity? All of the values of the soul will have been lost by the seekers of human praise. Not a vestige of value will remain to comfort one who has thus lived. The prize thus gained will have faded as a flower, and its momentary sweetness will yield to eternal bitterness.

There are but few passages in the Word of God that portray as well the inmost nature of man as does this one. It depicts him as he is, a lover of men rather than a lover of God. It shows him stooping toward the dust instead of reaching for the stars. He specializes in the microscope and discards the telescope; he settles for the values of the hour to the exclusion of the treasures of the ages.

What a tragedy that with Christ so near they chose to let Him pass! They seemed not to know that the Maker of all things was among them. They knew not His origin nor His destiny. They deemed Him to be passing, and His rewards temporary. So they chose to make no change, suffer no inconvenience, and endure no suffering. The god of this world had blinded their eyes, and the Man of sorrows moved on alone, to His cross and His crown.

But He Continued to Heal

When the Psalmist cried out, "Oh that men would praise the Lord for his goodness, and for his wonderful works to the children of men!" (Ps. 107:8, 15, 21, 31), He was appealing for that which is too often withheld, but which God does desire. The need for this exhortation is reflected in the fact that the exact words are used four times in the same chapter.

Praise is a form of worship, and the record is: "The true worshippers shall worship the Father in spirit and in truth: for the Father seeketh such to worship him" (John 4:23).

When Paul draws a picture of those upon whom "the wrath of God is revealed from heaven . . . because that, when they knew God, they glorified him not as God" (Rom. 1:18, 21), he further charged them as being unthankful. When we remember that every good and perfect gift comes from God, we should likewise know that the least that we can do in exchange for His free gifts is to praise and bless His name. To do less is gross ingratitude.

It is normal—even godlike—to desire gratitude from those to whom we render loving service or give unmerited gifts. When Jesus asked, "Where are the nine?" when only 1 of the 10 cleansed lepers returned to give Him thanks (Luke 17:11-19), He was expressing a yearning for appreciation. His suffering may have come more from the sin of the ungrateful 9 than from a personal slight, but regardless of the source, the fact remains that He felt the ingratitude and expressed His feelings.

13

While this is the only recorded instance where it is said that the healed did not return to give thanks, yet only a few times is there record that any did return to thank Him. Silence could mean that they did not return.

The main point of our message as suggested in the title is not to find fault with and condemn the unthankful, but rather to note the action of the Master in the light of such ingratitude.

It is natural for one to cease to help those who seem to have no appreciation for what is done for them, but that is not godlike. It is human, but not divine. Jesus kept on healing, gratitude or no gratitude. Blind Bartimaeus was not denied the healing touch for fear that he would be ungrateful.

Christ had come to exemplify the spirit and nature of God who "is kind unto the unthankful and to the evil" (Luke 6:35), and who sends His rain "on the just and on the unjust" (Matt 5:45). Jesus taught us to "do good, and lend, hoping for nothing again; and your reward shall be great, and ye shall be the children of the Highest" (Luke 6:35). The whole teaching of the Sermon on the Mount—in fact, the whole teaching of the gospel message—enjoins us to be good and to do good unselfishly, to bless those who curse us, and do good to those who despitefully use us.

We are reminded that if we lend, hoping to receive in return, we follow the pattern of the sinner. It is only when we give and lend, hoping for nothing in return, that we exemplify the spirit of the Lord who sends His rain on the just and on the unjust. Thus acting, one has the promise that "your reward shall be great, and ye shall be the children of the Highest."

The record is that "without faith it is impossible to please him" (Heb. 11:6); and perhaps nowhere does it require more faith to follow Him than when one is asked to keep on giving to the unthankful and to the evil.

At times, it appears that the more one does for another,

the less it is appreciated. The burning temptation is to quit. It seems to be the wise and natural thing to do. Why love when love is not returned? Why give when nothing is given in return? Why sacrifice for the thankless? Paul must have met this issue, for he lamented, "The more abundantly I love you, the less I be loved" (2 Cor. 12:15).

If the answer to these perplexing questions is strange, it is not therefore uncertain. We are to pursue this course of action that we may be the "children of the Highest." It is clear that God acts in this manner; that we cannot deny. He loved us when we despised Him. He blessed us when we cursed Him. He followed us when we ran from Him. He gave when we had nothing to return. It was this altruistic love that at last won our hearts. The goodness of God led us to repentance, and in our unselfish love lies the hope of bringing others to Him.

When it is promised, "Your reward shall be great," we are not told just what is involved in the promise. The complete revelation may be seen only in the world beyond, but an exhilarating foretaste comes when one sees some worn and benighted soul for whom he has shed tears, and to whom he has lent support, return to love and give thanks.

The thrill of the love of the loved, but once unloving, is heavenly. Just as the angelic joy over one penitent soul is more thrilling than that produced by the thought of 100 already saved, so likewise glorious is the love of one rescued wanderer.

The transformation of the selfish, unthankful soul into a loving and grateful spirit is so rewarding that the price paid to thus transform them is forgotten, submerged in love.

Lord, help me to become a child of the Highest by pouring out unrequited love and awaiting the great reward.

The Occasional Visitor
and
The Abiding Guest

Spread by centuries of time and divided at Pentecost stand two experiences represented by two passages of Scripture: (1) "God went up from Abraham" (Gen. 17:22); (2) "Lo, I am with you alway" (Matt. 28:20).

One cannot escape the thrill that comes from reviewing the life of that Old Testament saint, Abraham. He stands in a class alone; the high mountain of his journey must be seen by most of us only by telescope. He outdistanced his contemporaries and flagged his ascending path for all who care to follow.

When one reads, "And God said to Abraham," and then notes the clear, unambiguous leadings given him, it is exciting indeed!

To note the impossibles promised him (impossible with man, that is) and then note their every fulfillment, one finds himself breathing the ozone of another world and worshiping anew at the feet of the Holy one of Israel.

Upon close examination of the record, one disconcerting fact looms before us. Although God's visits were awe-inspiring, His messages unbelievable, and His identity undeniable, His visits seem to be few and far between. We must not and do not conclude that all of Abraham's contacts with God were made of record, but of this we are sure: He was not an abiding guest, for the record reads, "God went up from Abraham."

Such a visit was to be long remembered, for its message was awe-begetting, and the aura of His presence lingered as a beautiful dream. Weeks, months, even years were spent in meditations upon some of the divine messages before the promised fulfillment, and some even hung like meteors in the skies of centuries far away.

No shadow can bedim the glory of such moments of fellowship, and time could not erase their memories; but in spite of all this, the fact remains: "God went up"; He did not stay.

The pattern of Abraham's occasional rendezvous with his Lord is the universal pattern of pre-Pentecostal servants of the Lord. Although Jesus was with His own from their calling until He ascended, He was not with all people. His limitations were as ours—He could be in only one place at a time. He reminded His followers of the limitations of His day, telling them of the Spirit, "He dwelleth with you, and shall be in you" (John 14:17). He was with them in His power in the life of Christ, for "God was in Christ" (2 Cor. 5:19), but a better day would come. The limited outer would become the pervading inner. That is promised in our second verse of reference, "Lo, I am with you alway." Here the occasional becomes the permanent; the occasional Visitor has become the abiding Guest.

Pentecost made the difference, for Pentecost made possible the renovation of the human soul for fitness for the ever-indwelling Spirit.

It is not our purpose here to suggest why and how this was done. We desire only to underscore the fact that the Holy Spirit of Christ would be a permanent Guest in every Christian's heart and not an occasional Visitor standing at the tent's door.

17

Based upon the final completion of the Lamb's redemptive work accomplished at Calvary, and following and reaching final consummation and the approbation of the Father at Pentecost, the indwelling of the Spirit of God was made possible.

No longer does a child of God need to wait for years, as did Abraham, for an intimate interview with His Father and His Son through the Spirit. He would be an abiding Guest, a conversing Guest, and not a silent one.

If the revelations made to our father Abraham were breathtaking (and they were), when they were occasional only, how much more thrilling the constant revelations available to the saint from the Spirit's indwelling!

Paul tells us, "Eye hath not seen, nor ear heard . . . the things which God hath prepared for them that love him" (1 Cor. 2:9). But the apostle does not stop here on this negative note, but soars to a glorious, positive one: "But God hath revealed them unto us by his Spirit" (v. 10). What in the Old Testament was an occasional revelation may become a constant and endless one.

Let no one think that the supply will run out. The God who peopled the firmament with countless suns and gave to each of His children a personal, unerasable, and unduplicated fingerprint, will never run out of material to reveal, and He is pledged to do it. The Spirit, Jesus said, has access to all that the Father has, and stands ready to reveal it to those who meet the divine conditions of knowing.

There is a diet for all ages of Christians, from the milk-drinking octogenarian-infant to the mature, meat-eating youngster. The glorious thing about all this is that Jesus is glorified when the Holy Spirit shows His followers the things that belong to Him.

In the light of all this truth, and in full view of all of God's riches, we must bow our heads in shame and ask, "Why are we so poorly fed? Why are we so ignorant?"

The answer is clear and convicting; we must seek this as silver, and search for it as for hidden treasure. The passion of our souls must be as that of Paul: "I count all things but loss . . . that I may know him" (Phil. 3:8, 10). Nothing less than this earnestness can make it safe for God to reveal himself to us. He will not cast His pearls before swine, nor give himself and His things to those who have no proper appreciation for them.

Our paucity of divine truth cannot be charged to His unwillingness nor to our inability, but to our lack of desire for and appreciation of Him and His.

Am I?

In the midst of the swirling, foaming vortex of human history there stands a lighthouse whose foundation is immovable and whose light is unquenchable. "Then spake Jesus again unto them, saying, I am the light of the world" (John 8:12). "His life is the light that shines through the darkness—and the darkness can never extinguish it" (1:5, TLB). "That was the true Light, which lighteth every man that cometh into the world" (v. 9).

This light of Christ's was not inherently His but had been given to Him by the Father. It was the shining forth of life—the life of the Father that had been given to the Son, for "God was in Christ" (2 Cor. 5:19). He clearly stated the source of the life that radiated light through Him to the world when He said, "For as the Father hath life in himself; so hath he given to the Son to have life in himself" (John 5:26).

He did claim, "I am the resurrection, and the life" (11:25); however, this claim does in no way invalidate His statement that this life and light had been given to Him by the Father.

That the light that was in Christ was a radiation from the life that was in Him is clearly stated in His words, "He that followeth me shall not walk in darkness, but shall have the light of life" (John 8:12). It was the life that was in Christ that was the source of the light that He was, and that life—the source of that light—was given to Him by the Father.

Although the Spirit of Christ had worked through the consciences of all men (for He was that "true Light, which lighteth every man that cometh into the world" [John 1:9]), nevertheless, until He came in the flesh, there had not been a perfect embodiment of the life of God radiating throughout the world. The coming of this light-radiating life was in the incarnation period and was limited thereto. These statements of Christ bear this out:

"And this is the condemnation, that light is come into the world, and men loved darkness rather than light, because their deeds were evil" (John 3:19).

"I am come a light into the world" (12:46).

This points to the definite time of His coming as the light. That He would not thus light the world after His going away is evident from His statement, "As long as I am in the world, I am the light of the world" (John 9:5). His ability to light the world in the way that He was then lighting it was limited to His stay on the earth.

There is a parallel to this in another area, the account given in 2 Cor. 5:18-20. The apostle pictures God as working through Christ while He was upon earth, reconciling the world unto himself; but upon His departure, He committed the work of reconciliation to His followers: "Christ . . . hath given to us the ministry of reconciliation; . . . Now then we are ambassadors for Christ, as though God did beseech you by us: we pray you in Christ's stead, be ye reconciled to God" (vv. 18, 20).

The work of reconciliation was Christ's while He was upon earth, and upon His departure He gave this task to His followers. In like manner, when Christ went away, He gave the task of bearing light to the world to His followers. He told them, "Ye are the light of the world" (Matt. 5:14). Elsewhere He stated, "I am the light of the world," and now He reminds them, "Ye are the light of the world."

How can it be that we are the same thing that He said himself to be—the light of the world? We can better under-

21

stand how we can become the light of the world when we remember how He became the light of the world.

We have already noted that this light in Him that was produced by the life that was in Him was not inherent, but was given to Him by the Father. When we understand that the Christ who had no life and light in himself received it from Another, we may then understand better how we, His followers, possessed of no life and light of our own, may receive such from Him and thus become in His own words, "the light of the world."

No longer is it God shining through the Man Christ Jesus, giving life and light to the world, but it is Christ giving life and light to the world through His followers, as the Father had done through Him.

There is another parallel thought brought out by Jesus when He said, "As my Father hath sent me, even so send I you" (John 20:21).

The sending power of the Father sustained the Son in all of His work, and by the same token the sending power of Christ can sustain those whom He sends. We may thus assume that we have the same backing that Jesus had as we carry out His will upon earth.

The evidences pile up: As God sent Christ, so Christ sends us; as God was reconciling through Christ, so Christ would reconcile through us; and as Christ was the Light of the World in the days of His flesh, so we are to be the light of the world in His absence.

We come now to the question of the message. Are we the light of the world? Am I?

It is easy to shift the responsibility to the corporate whole—to say that the Church is the light of the world. Yes, that is true, but the Church is made up of individuals, and no number of assembled persons with unlit candles can become a light. The responsibility must, therefore, rest upon each individual. So the question is pertinent—Am I? Am *I* a light of the world? This question must be answered affirmatively and personally before it can become effective collectively.

Am I a light? Am I the kind of light that Jesus was? The light that He was, was disturbing. He was a problem to His age, a disturber of the status quo. The disturbance grew out of the fact that He was the Light that was on the candlestick and not under the bushel; He shone forth and lighted the lives of those about Him. The hypocrisy of the Pharisees was illuminated, and they were determined to put Him to death. He testified that some "men loved darkness rather than light, because their deeds were evil. For every one that doeth evil hateth the light, neither cometh to the light, lest his deeds should be reproved" (John 3:19-20).

The picture of the world is that it is both evil and asleep, and it is very distasteful to a sleeping child to have a bright light thrown on his face. Thus the light-bearer has always been an object of hatred. Jesus affirmed, "If the world hate you, ye know that it hated me before it hated you" (John 15:18).

Perhaps here we have one reason why the light of our lives shines so dimly. There is suffering for the one that brings light, for in many cases, light is not wanted. The deeds of men are evil, and they do not want light thrown upon them. Then the pressure is brought upon the light-bearer to tone down the light, reduce the wattage, or cover it with a bushel. John the Baptist faced this problem but kept his light brightly burning until the axman extinguished it.

Christ dealt only in the truth. He clung to the light, for in Him "is no darkness at all" (1 John 1:5). It was the light of His life that nailed Him to the Cross.

The question again: Am I? Am I a light, and if so, is it on a candlestick or under the bushel? The lack of disturbance that my life causes may be the answer here. If my life and ministry cause no furor, provoke no carnally minded, challenge no rebellious soul, arouse no opposition, then I must

23

say, "My candle is burning low or is well-nigh hidden. In either event, I am a poor representative of my Master, who carried His light to the Cross and beamed it out in 'Father, forgive them; for they know not what they do' (Luke 23:34)."

Stephen's light shone brilliantly unto the very end, and the last rays of his candle were penetrating: "Lord, lay not this sin to their charge" (Acts 7:60). This last sharp beam struck deep into the heart of the arch-persecutor and brought him to a more brilliant light on the Damascus road. Stephen died in the doing, but he lives in his deed.

The question might well be put to myself in this way: "Am I willing and ready to offer my life for the Master and those for whom He died? Am I willing to 'lay down [my life] for the brethren' (1 John 3:16)?"

Lord, Thou knowest that twice in my life I have offered Thee my life for the soul of another. Thou didst not take it, but the offer was sincere. That Thou knowest. My life is in Thy hands to be sacrificed upon any altar if that can bring glory to Thy name.

May I close this meditation with a prayer for a specific cause. *A cargo is drifting toward ruin. If in this effort it would please Thee to take my life and save the precious cargo, I gladly offer it to Thee. I have no hesitancy in doing it, for I know Thou wilt do what is best for all involved, and I want nothing but Thy best.*

Thou didst give Thy life for me. I gladly give my life to Thee for whatever disposition Thou dost care to make of it. I love Thee supremely, and it would be a thrill to see Thee face-to-face this very night. I could meet Thee in peace, knowing that to the best of my ability I have sought to follow Thee fully.

Good-night, Lord, until it will be Good morning.

Amen.

I Can Be Honest

I can't be wise, I can't be great, and there are many other things I just cannot be, and there is no need to pretend that I am or can be; but of one thing I am absolutely certain, *I can be honest!* There is no power but my own that can keep me from thus being, so I can if I will, and I affirm that I will.

This way of honesty is not native to me. I was a born liar. I was born of my father, the devil, and he was a liar from the beginning. All of his children have inherited this trait. In some it is more pronounced than in others, but it is present in all. Hence the divine command—"Ye must be born again," born from above (John 3:7).

It is not easy to define the word *lying*. Because of this, we often hear the expressions "a bold-faced liar," a "little lie," a "white lie," and so on. Then there is the practice of telling less than the whole truth, leaving an incorrect conception by omission of segments of truth. Overconscientious persons are accused at times by the adversary because they do not give all the facts of the story, when there are times when all the facts *should not* be told. At times, Jesus did not give all the facts to the disciples. To withhold facts or parts of the facts is not necessarily to lie, but to say no when the truth is yes is to lie, and "all liars, shall have their part in the lake which burneth with fire and brimstone" (Rev. 21:8).

There is one area where it is difficult to be frank and honest, for the truth and facts seem to reflect upon God and destroy what people call their faith. It is in this area that I wish to speak.

A good example (and there are others) is our claim of divine healing where there is none. I have thought on and studied this problem for many years—over 50—and am of the firm belief that we are weak in our healing ministry because we claim healings that are not real, and believe that we have such power with God when we have not, and thus falsely believing, we do not get to reality.

When I have faced this matter in judgment-day honesty, and have had the courage to tell the simple, unvarnished truth as I see it, it shakes many people, and I have been accused of destroying the people's faith. My answer to that is, The truth cannot destroy faith. Jesus never destroyed the faith of anyone, but He dealt in truth. He shook people—crumbled their sandy foundations, but pointed them to the rock of faith on which their house could be safely built.

Before going further, and lest I be misunderstood, let me affirm that I am a strong believer in miraculous divine healing, the kind of which the Bible gives account—blinded eyes opened, paralyzed limbs instantly healed, deaf ears unstopped, withered arms restored to normalcy instantly. I believe the accounts of those things as recorded in the Book, and I believe that such healings and miracles are within the realm of faith. I further believe that God would be glorified and His kingdom speedily advanced today if such supernatural works were done among us. All this I steadfastly believe is well supported by the Word of God.

Against the background of this sincere belief as to what might and should be, I honestly state what I have seen—or rather, have *not* seen in this field.

May I, for emphasis, put it this way: If I were standing before Jesus Christ, my Judge, on the day of final judgment, and He were to say to me, "T. W. Willingham, you are before Me for your final judgment. I will pronounce it today, and it will be final and forever." Then He would draw aside two curtains, one opening vistas to the city of light with all that we know of heaven, and the other revealing the regions of the lost in all of their divinely revealed horror. Then, when I had viewed them fairly, He would say to me, "Your eternal destiny will be in one of these two places, and this will be the deciding factor: I will not consider a word or an act of your life; I will base My final judgment on your answer to one question. If you lie, you will be sent to hell. If you tell the truth, I will send you to heaven."

Certainly one would be inclined to be honest on such an occasion!

Then would come the question: "Did you ever in all of your lifetime, according to your present recollection, see any act of healing in the flesh of man that you, as an observer (by observation alone and not by the testimony of another), could say was without reasonable doubt a miraculous act of Mine?"

Then I would answer, "Jesus, You know the answer to that question as well as I do, and You know that I speak the truth when I say, I have not!"

Then with the upward wave of His hand, He would respond, "Enter thou into the joy of thy Lord."

. Let me add, it will do no good for anyone to rush up and give me the account of your great healing. I do not deny any healing that anyone professes to have had. I am only testifying to what I have not seen, and your testimony would not in any way alter mine.

I have been in our church over 70 years, traveled in all of the continental states, and ministered in many churches and camps from ocean to ocean. I have seen thousands anointed for healing and have heard many testimonies of physical help. I do not question these testimonies, but I repeat, I have never witnessed any organic healing that, as an observer, I could believe that God did.

If there had been many such healings, I believe I would

have seen at least one. I lament that my testimony is as it is, but I would be a liar if I were to change it.

I revert to an earlier statement. I think there should be Bible-like cases of healings—healings that no honest person could deny—and I believe if we would face our failures frankly, that it would open the way for new light and help. As long as we claim that we have arrived, we will not seek to go forward. It is in the interest of the real that I thus speak. May we face the issue honestly and seek divine help.

I Have Listened

For some time now I have been listening to the "still small voice" concerning my writing. Several times He has asked, "Would you like to write?" When I have responded, I have been able to write with ease and without hesitancy. This is the second four-page chapter that I have written since 9:30 tonight.

This is very encouraging to me, for I often begin at once on a subject that I had never had in mind. Another wonderful thing about it is that it has always worked. Just minutes ago I started this chapter, and as of this second, I don't know what more to say; but if it turns out to be as at other times, I will finish it without extra thought and with no hesitation.

This listening has been a matter of my life's study. I have always (since being saved) believed in a speaking God. At times He speaks concerning the ordinary; at other times His message is contrary to the standards set by men, even Christian men. I reserve the right to listen to Him and obey Him even if His leadings are contrary to the opinion of others. The only question of my asking is, "Is it God?" Settle that and obedience will follow. I confess that when the command is not in line with the standard and conventional, I make a more diligent inquiry as to the Speaker; but I will not deny that He can make himself known—known so certainly that the humanly impossible can be done at His bidding! In fact, if there is not something accomplished that human hands cannot perform, there is little use of calling it God. I am sure that God would like to see things done through His children that His children cannot do of themselves. Then it will be that He, and not the children, can be praised.

If there are to be such acts performed—acts of divine stature—they must be done at His command; hence the importance of listening. "Faith cometh by hearing" (Rom. 10:17) and in no other way, and one can't do much hearing unless he listens. Listening, therefore, is important—in fact, imperative!

Since there is nothing too hard for God, and since God can order His humanly impossible tasks to be performed by His servants if He so wills and orders, it is necessary for His will to be made known. Unbelief cannot hear His voice; only to men of faith does He speak understandingly. Thus, faith must embrace the possibility of the impossible and be ready to act in the realm of the impossible when such orders come. If such humanly impossible tasks are not considered possible, the Voice requiring them will not be heeded.

It is needless to say that there are conditions to be met if one would hear the Voice. First, there must be a passion to know His will. This bespeaks our own insufficiency and His enabling. Then there must be, along with the desire to know, the equally strong purpose to obey.

There can be no substitute for obedience, and obedience must be full and complete. There is no reason to seek to hear if there is no purpose to obey. The will to do must precede the knowing.

"I have listened" is my testimony. This listening has not been perfect, but it has been more or less constant; and through the years it has become more and more the pattern of my life, until now it is becoming a consuming passion.

When I think of our trial-and-error methods born of our own ignorance, and then think of His infinite wisdom offered to all, I am amazed at our own lack of listening for His will to be made known.

I am practicing the listening. This little article is another test case. It was started with only a heading in mind, and here it is developing; less than two minutes have been lost since the first word was penned. No stopping, no extra thought, no effort. Virtually all my writing has been of this nature. Thus saying, I am not charging God with all that I write. I invoke one of my own sayings at this point: "When God and I work together, the end product will not be perfect. It will have the gold of the divine and the dross of the human."

The point at issue is that when I have heard the Voice, I have been able to write without loss of time and with ease. Such ease comes at no other time; therefore I listen for the Voice.

I have not always listened; I have been consumed with my own thinking. Wondering just how this or that will sound when read, and just how it will meet with approval. When I follow the Voice, I think nothing of man's approval or disapproval. If the Voice is from God, He will back His own Voice. That He has done for months and is doing now.

It certainly is reasonable to believe that He has not lost His ability to speak. He had such ability once. That we know if we accept the Word as His. If it could be proven that He could no longer speak, we would have grounds to forsake Him; or if it could be proven that He no longer cared to speak, then our interest in Him would be lessened if not destroyed.

I affirm, "I have listened"; and with equal force I affirm, "I have heard Him speak." He speaks to me often and about many things. I listen for His Voice. It is always reliable and available. "My sheep hear my voice" (John 10:27) was not for the ancients alone; it is for the sheep of today's pasture. I affirm His speaking to me, and by that Voice I would be guided.

This Voice is not a substitute for His written Word—by no means! Hearing comes by "the word of God"—the written Word and also by His spoken word. They are complimentary and never contradictory. To revel in His Word makes the Voice possible.

Do We Look for Another?

Of all the prophets whose messages came thundering from the past, one would least expect an expression of doubt from the one who uttered the question, "Do we look for another?" (Matt. 11:3).

John the Baptist, the rough-spoken, camel-skin-clad, locust-eating recluse, ascended his wilderness pulpit and shouted in stentorian voice, "Behold the Lamb of God, which taketh away the sin of the world" (John 1:29).

So loud and assuring was his message that "there went out unto him all the land of Judaea, and they of Jerusalem, and were all baptized of him . . . confessing their sins" (Mark 1:5).

He declared with unflinching dogmatism the coming of the Messiah and demanded that every valley be filled, every mountain and hill be brought low, and the crooked and rough ways be made straight and smooth for the oncoming Redeemer.

He castigated the sinning Pharisees and Sadducees by calling them a "generation of vipers" and demanded them to "bring forth . . . fruits meet for repentance" (Matt 3:7-8). The Lamb would lay the ax at the root of the trees, and the fruitless one would be cut down and burned. The wheat and chaff would be separated, and the chaff burned "with unquenchable fire" (v. 12).

So certain was the prophet that he was heralding the Holy One of Israel that he deemed himself unworthy to loosen the latchet of His shoes.

Perhaps never before had there come a prophetic message so thunderous and so certain as the fearless Baptist proclaimed beyond the Jordan. It had the backing of the ancient writers, the evident blessing from above, and all the vigor of a divine ambassador dedicated to his heaven-given mission.

Who could believe that this stalwart preacher—this unbroken reed—could be bent and bruised and his own message brought into question by himself? Could the cloud of doubt bedim such brilliant light? Could that stentorian voice be smothered to a faint whisper? Could that towering faith totter in the winds of adversity?

Alas, such was the case. The freedom of the desert had been exchanged for the chains of a dank prison cell, and the massive throngs of his former ministry for a lone Roman sentinel. His solitude was depressing, his dream unrealized, his Hero disappointing; the promised ax was not evident. No rising smoke from burning chaff could be seen. The Lamb had not removed the sin of the world—not even the sin of an unjust judge who had committed His forerunner to prison. Doubt was eclipsing faith.

The question was inevitable. Have I been mistaken in my message? Have I announced a false Deliverer? John thought, "I will put the question to Him squarely: 'Art thou he that should come, or do we look for another?'"

This was a question packed with pathos, loaded with grief, and stained with the tears of a storm-tossed soul. An answer there must be! A quivering soul demanded it; a just God could not withhold it. It came, and with it, peace.

As meaningful as this experience was to the Baptist, we shall not pursue that phase of the story but rather seek to draw from it some lessons for our own lives.

If God had not inspired the record, the low place in the Baptist's faith might have gone unrecorded; but the divine historian does not mar the true portrait by an essential omission. We need to know that the stalwarts of faith and action had their weak moments, and that cloudless skies were not always their heritage.

God has a way of overshadowing our paths with darkness, giving us courage through the weaknesses of others, helping us to realize that when we are weak, then are we strong.

The flickering torch of the wilderness preacher lights our way and makes firmer our grip on our windswept candle. We gather hope from the tested pilgrim who emerges from the dense forest still pressing onward and upward. The light of the day is more brilliant against the darkness of the night just past, and hope mounts higher as it faces the next encounter.

We, like the Baptist, have not seen our dreams fulfilled as we so boldly acclaimed. The path to fulfillment has not always been understood. Too often we have demanded to see in time that which can only be clear in eternity. We fail to remember that God operates in two worlds, while we are confined to only one. It takes faith to wait for the mansion in the sky as we behold the hovels in the valley. We long for maturity without growth, wisdom without teaching, perfection without temptation, Christlikeness without suffering.

What then are the lessons that come to us from the Baptist?

First: The one sent of God does not always clearly see the end of his mission. He may see only the seed; the flower and the fruit may be that of others.

Second: The adversities that come to the servant of God are not necessarily the marks of divine disfavor.

Third: Righteousness is proclaimed expensively. Sinning Herods still behead the prophets, and light-rejecting professors still cry, "Crucify Him."

Fourth: When our soul-rocking question is frankly asked, the quiet and certain answer of the Master is soon forthcoming, and it always bears the marks of His compassion and love.

Fifth: The blood-stained walls where Christians die have challenged to heroism countless others and given credence to the agelong verdict, "The blood of the martyrs is the seed of the Church."

Sixth: The eulogy of the Master sent to the royal prisoner was enough to make his rocky pallet seem a pad of softest down.

Seventh: The martyr's crown has been guaranteed: "If we suffer, we shall also reign with him" (2 Tim. 2:12).

The suffering and the rejoicing cannot be divorced. I accept both.

Save Yourselves

"Save yourselves." Yes, that is the commandment from the Word of God. I had thought that Christ was to do all the saving, and lo and behold, the responsibility is thrown back on me: "Save yourselves"!

What does this mean in the light of the fact that "there is none other name under heaven given among men, whereby we must be saved" but the name of Jesus (Acts 4:12)? In what sense does He save, and in what sense must I save myself? If I am responsible for saving myself, then I must not cast all the responsibility on Christ and then, in the end, blame Him if I am lost.

There is certainly a saving that only Christ can do, but likewise, there is a saving that only I can do. The fuller statement from which our theme is taken was used by Peter on the Day of Pentecost: "Save yourselves from this untoward generation" (Acts 2:40). Here is a saving that Christ cannot do for us. He has commanded us to "come out from among them, and be ye separate" (2 Cor. 6:17). This is something that Christ cannot do. He was not "among them" in the first place. We were, or are, among them; hence, we are the only ones who can "come out."

In a like vein, we are commanded to "work out [our] own salvation with fear and trembling" (Phil. 2:12). This, God cannot do for us; we are commanded to do it ourselves. The implantation of salvation within us is the part of God. The working out of that which He has implanted within us is ours to do; therefore, it is said, "It is God which worketh in you both to will and to do of his good pleasure" (v. 13). It is His part to light the candle in the soul, but the manner and the place of the shining forth is left to us; hence, we are commanded to keep it on a candlestick and not under a bushel.

This working out of our salvation is a lifelong process. It begins with the inception of spiritual life and should continue to the end of life's day—and for aught we know, even through all eternity.

If it is asked, How may this working out of this implanted salvation be done? The answer is that it can only be done in the spirit and with the aid of Him who implanted it in the first place. That brings us face-to-face with the spirit of the Master, and that spirit is clearly delineated in the Word of God, which amply reflects the acts of His life, the spirit behind those acts, and the priorities that He announced as fitting—yea, even necessary.

Just turn to His picture for guidance, and here is what we find. The driving motive that moved Him through life was an absolute and complete acceptance of, and obedience to, the will of His Father. With Christ there was no substitute for obedience, and there can be none for us if we are to follow Him. He repeatedly emphasized this, and in terms that no intelligent person can deny. He reminded His followers that they need not call Him "Lord" and do not the things that He had commanded them.

The necessity of obedience is indispensable to the destruction of the central sin of the human heart—the sin that divided the heavens before man was formed, and which spread as an eating cancer throughout the whole of the human race. It is the tacit acknowledgment of the fact that there is a supreme, superior Being to whom we owe allegiance and love. By this law of obedience, and by it alone, can harmony come in the universe. The heart of sin is self-will. The center of righteousness is divine will. Christ came to recognize this principle and to exemplify it in the most positive way—the way of obedience unto death.

In yielding in unlimited obedience to the Father, He did, by the same act, yield himself to all of the ordinances of man established within the framework of the Father's announced plan. He was never a rebel. He respected the laws and rules that His Father had established for men. His answer to those who would direct Him otherwise was "It becometh us to fulfil all righteousness" (Matt. 3:15).

Often on His lips were the words "It is written"; and when He found that word, His path was clear, and for Him there was no other way. The "written" must be carried out.

In one of His darkest moments, when from some source the suggestion came to change His course of action, He answered, "But how then shall the scriptures be fulfilled . . . ?" (Matt. 26:54). He had come to fulfill, and not to destroy, the law. He challenged the hypocrite who, under the guise of obeying a higher law of God, disobeyed the law of man that had been ordained of God.

Christ assured us that God is not a thief. He would not take from Caesar that which belonged to him, and thus speaking, He acknowledged that there were some things that belonged to Caesar; they had been given to him by His Father, and He would not rob him of them.

He told His followers to heed the commands of the priests, for they sat in Moses' seat, but they were not to do as they did; for they said but did not. His respect was for the God-made law, even though those who were administering it might be crooked.

He announced the priority of the spiritual over the material, asking "What is a man profited, if he shall gain the whole world, and lose his own soul?" (Matt. 16:26). With this one unanswerable question He set the eternal above the temporal forever and enjoined His followers to do likewise. He affirmed that the love of money is the root of all evil, and that man is only a steward of what he possesses, and that a certain reckoning day is coming. He invited all to lay up treasures in heaven, and thus speaking, proclaimed the safety of the heavenly vaults as against those of earth that are often pilfered.

Jesus recognized that His Spirit was in opposition to the spirit of the age in which He lived. If His followers were to live with Him eternally, they must save themselves from the world. He reminded them that they were not of the world, even as He was not of the world. If they were to be true followers of His, they must catch this other-world spirit and be willing to suffer the reproach that inevitably comes to one who dares to be different. It was this likeness to Him, which was unlikeness to the world, that would cause the inevitable suffering of which He was telling them. If, then, they were to follow Him, they must accept His cross and follow Him to the end.

If His followers were to save themselves in the sense that He required, that salvation must be in the world to come; hence they were not to look for salvation in this life in the sense that men of the world looked for it. They might, in saving their lives eternally, lose them in time. Here is where His teaching appears concerning the value of the eternal as contrasted with the temporal.

The follower of Christ, the one who truly saves himself, must have been taken out of this world, not in body, but in spirit. Jesus prayed, "Not that thou shouldest take them out of the world" (John 17:15). He also said, "They are not of the world" (v. 16). Here we have references to the body and to the spirit. Concerning their bodies, Jesus referred to His followers as "these [that] are in the world" (v. 11). When referring to their spirits, He said, "They are not of the world, even as I am not of the world." The disciples must carry a foreign spirit while living upon the earth. The whole world lieth in the wicked one, and the Christian is in Christ. The two are at variance; "therefore the world hateth you" (15:19).

In saving oneself, one must accept this discord between his spirit and the spirit of the age. These spirits are diametrically opposed to each other. They cannot be harmonized, and it is futile and fatal to attempt it. "Ye cannot serve God and mammon" (Matt. 6:24). The Christian must acknowledge this basic and inevitable antagonism, and accept the consequences of it gladly as for Christ's sake, as indeed it is.

To save oneself, there must be an unshakable faith that the world beyond, for which he has forsaken all to attain, is indeed and in truth a place, a place prepared for him, a place eternal in the heavens. If there is any uncertainty at this point, he will never sacrifice the visible for the invisible and will continue to walk by sight and not by faith, and will, in the end, perish.

Lastly, if one would save himself, he must have companionship as he journeys this upward way. He cannot make it alone. Christ recognized this necessity and told His followers, "I will not leave you comfortless" (John 14:18).

The presence of the Comforter not only guarantees guidance, which Jesus promised that He would give, but His presence is a constant proof of another world, for He is so completely different from any spirit of this world that it is apparent that He came from another world; so there must be another world from which He came. Following Him, we will indeed save ourselves eternally.

We Are Appointed Thereunto

Would you deliberately, without just reason, break an appointment with your dearest friend who had come from afar to visit you? Suppose you had an appointment with the governor of your state, or the president of the United States, would you willingly break it?

Is it not true that in proportion as one values the friendship and esteems the importance of the one with whom he has an appointment, in the same proportion will he seek to keep that appointment? The higher our esteem, the more careful are we to meet our friend at the appointed time.

It follows in the thinking of all rational beings that an appointment set up with God at His request is by far the most important. He has made more than one such appointment, some of which we cannot fail to meet. The meeting is predetermined, and to keep the engagement is no matter of choice with us. Neither the fact of the appointment nor its time or place is determined by us. Such are the twin appointments of death and the judgment. "It is appointed unto men once to die, but after this the judgment" (Heb. 9:27). Meet these man must; he has no choice.

However, there are other appointments whose keeping is optional with us. God cannot enforce the keeping on our part. Such is the nature of the one under discussion here. It would seem that many, if not most, Christians draw back from this appointment. Some even break with Christ rather than to meet it. When asked why such reluctance, we must answer that it does not always arise from the same source. Any refusal to meet this divine appointment is unacceptable, but where there is no positive refusal there is often unnecessary hesitancy. To help to overcome this reluctance, this chapter is being sent your way.

To put the matter in its clear perspective, it must be established that it is a divine appointment. When this is made clear, the way for action is clearly opened. This appointment, the one now being introduced, is a divine one. There can be no question here. It is made by God himself for all of His children. The call is clear and oft repeated. It is the call to suffering. Paul exhorts, "That no man should be moved by these afflictions: for yourselves know that we are appointed thereunto" (1 Thess. 3:3).

One should not be sidetracked by the thought that the apostle was speaking of some "affliction" peculiar to the ones to whom he was writing, and having no message for all Christians. It could well be that this particular affliction was peculiar to them, but even so, it was but typical of the universal application of this call to suffer. It is a well-established appointment, as the following testimonies confirm.

On other occasions—"at Antioch, at Iconium, at Lystra" (2 Tim. 3:11)—Paul was "confirming the souls of the disciples, and exhorting them to continue in the faith, and that we must through much tribulation enter into the kingdom of God" (Acts 14:22).

Speaking of Christian suffering, Peter reminds us that, "hereunto were ye called: because Christ also suffered for us, leaving us an example, that ye should follow his steps" (1 Pet. 2:21).

Jesus too made the matter perfectly clear: "In the world ye shall have tribulation" (John 16:33), and "The servant is not greater than his lord. If they have persecuted me, they will also persecute you" (15:20).

42

No call of God is made more clear in His Word than the Christian's call to suffer with Christ. When the true Christian fully realizes this, he more readily accepts this appointment and, in fact, welcomes it. He greets it as a moment of triumph, for glory and reward attend it; it is written, "If we suffer, we shall also reign with him" (2 Tim. 2:12). His path to glory was one of suffering, and ours cannot be otherwise.

The call to holiness ("without which no man shall see the Lord" [Heb. 12:14]) is a call to suffering. They cannot be separated. The one springs from the other. In fact, it is holiness that produces suffering of the type under consideration. Hear Jesus on the subject: "If ye were of the world, the world would love his own: but because ye are not of the world, but I have chosen you out of the world, therefore the world hateth you" (John 15:19).

Suffering is inherent in holiness just as much as heat is inherent in fire, and cold inherent in ice. To be holy is to suffer, and to dodge suffering is to forfeit holiness. It is that simple.

Let those who share no suffering examine their relationship with the sufferers, for "all that will live godly in Christ Jesus shall suffer persecution" (2 Tim. 3:12). Note the "all" and the "shall." The universality and certainty are well established but not for all who profess to be Christians, but for those "that will live godly in Christ Jesus." Here is the tape line. Let God measure you, and it would be well to "examine yourselves, whether ye be in the faith" (2 Cor. 13:5).

When one can see the divineness of the call and its reward, he can better understand what James is talking about when he writes, "Count it all joy when ye fall into divers temptations" (1:2).

Peter had found the value in suffering, and exhorted, "Rejoice, inasmuch as ye are partakers of Christ's sufferings; that, when his glory shall be revealed, ye may be glad also with exceeding joy" (1 Pet. 4:13).

43

All the apostles saw the inevitableness of suffering if one would be Christlike; they saw the coming joy that outweighed the suffering, and could shout in triumph, "For our light affliction, which is but for a moment, worketh for us a far more exceeding and eternal weight of glory" (2 Cor. 4:17).

It was for "the joy . . . set before him" that Jesus "endured the cross" and despised its shame, that He might have a seat at the Father's right hand (Heb. 12:2). To go this way one must have faith in God—faith that all that He promises His suffering saints will come true; for "without faith it is impossible to please him" (11:6), but with faith one can live his life, suffer the cross, endure the pain, and reign with Him forever. "Comfort one another with these words" (1 Thess. 4:18).

In the Medley of Madness I Heard a Voice

"The medley of madness"—where could that be? Really, that is not the proper question. The correct question is, Where on the inhabited earth may one go where there is *not* a medley of voices? To make the matter worse, the voices are in conflict; and (face it frankly) they are not only in conflict, but they are in many instances hostile.

One glance at a news digest confirms this affirmation. Long ago Isaiah saw man's sad plight and wrote, "All we like sheep have gone astray; we have turned every one to his own way" (Isa. 53:6). Here is God's picture of man's fallen plight: no unity, no peace, no cooperation; each on his own, going "his own way"!

The medley of madness is everywhere, but it was in this medley that I heard a voice; I first heard it when I was a small lad. It came to me in the silence of the eventide. It came again and again. At last I listened. It was soft, tender, and wooing. Its cadence was unlike the disturbing din of the raucous throng. Its call was to rest. I listened, I heeded, I found, and I am happy.

I have found what the mad, clamoring multitude can never find. I found rest in the midst of the tumult, rest in the fury of the storm. Strange as it may seem, I found it not by struggling, not by demanding, but by surrender, for thus does life begin.

45

Through the years I have turned my hearing aid to the tones of the Voice, the Voice unlike that of any of the wild, maddening crowd—the Voice of calm, the Voice of power, the Voice of peace.

This maddened age is crying for peace but feverishly preparing for war. It hopes to find peace when peace comes to the world. The sober fact is that there is no peace coming—not this side of the coming of Him who is the Prince of Peace. The mad rush for universal peace is futile, but for the Christian it is not necessary. It would be enjoyable, but it is not required. The Master's words "Be of good cheer" were spoken against the background of His declaration, "In the world ye shall have tribulation" (John 16:33).

The peace that Jesus gives may be received by anyone at any time and enjoyed everywhere at all times.

The Voice I hear amid the deadening din is one of quietness. Its piercing note penetrates the noise of tumult, and its message comes through without distortion. This Voice gives direction as well as peace. It points to a safe but narrow way through all the divergent paths. It speaks at the intersections and indicates the turns.

To add to the medley of madness by worldlings, there is the medley of ignorance from well-meaning friends. One beckons for speed, and another for caution. One points to the east, and another to the west. If there were no Voice, who would guide?

There is a marked difference between the voices of others and the voice of my Shepherd. The voice of the Shepherd often calls to paths on which I find no recent footprints. Friends would cry, "Unsafe," "Unorthodox"; and some would even cry, "Unchristian." Under such circumstances, I check the voice with care; I know there is a ventriloquist and an aper as well. He has deceived many and is bent on deceiving all, even the elect. I then check and recheck and double-check.

While the Voice may lead counter to the conventional, He never leads contrary to the written; and with all of His leadings, He gives double assurance, accompanied by peace.

I have checked this Voice and will continue to do so. He demands no haste born of uncertainty and casts no shadow over one's tender conscience. All He asks is attention, nearness, and obedience. These granted, He makes himself known, and reality marks His every move. The heart is light and carefree. The whole being is full of light and life. Each dawning day brings new vistas and the assurance that the way is more pleasant as the journey continues.

"The sheep . . . know his voice. And a stranger will they not follow" (John 10:4-5). There need be no fear of the Shepherd's voice if one carries the constant assurance that he belongs to the great Shepherd's fold. Such assurance is available for us all. The promise is "The Spirit itself beareth witness with our spirit, that we are the children of God" (Rom. 8:16).

"Try the spirits" is a divine injunction (1 John 4:1). The speaking Voice welcomes investigation. Mark up the messages that come through the throng; check their fulfillment. If they are false, the voice was false. Check again and again. By constant application one comes to discern "both good and evil" (Heb. 5:14), and by the same token, he comes to understand the Voice.

The way ahead has never been trodden by us. The way taken by most Christians does not lead to the better treasures of the Master. New paths must be entered; a new Voice must be heard, or the voice of the Speaker comprehended more clearly. All this argues for a closer walk with the Speaker, an ear more deaf to the noises of the rabble, a casual listening to all the speakers, and a passionate longing to hear the clear, soft tones of the loving Shepherd's voice.

Our listening must be constant, our obedience complete, and our ear ever turned toward Him. To start the perilous path at His call requires constant contact for successful completion.

Peter heard the "come" and started, but was not constant in the looking and began to sink. His cry for mercy was heard. Learn by His mistake. Go at the Shepherd's call but be open for His orders, and all will be well.

Sit Down
in the Lowest Room

(Luke 14:10)

When Jesus advised a man who was invited to a wedding supper to "sit down in the lowest room," He was but introducing him to a chapter of His own autobiography and suggesting that the life story of the invited guest be patterned after that of His own.

The Good Shepherd's "follow me" is clearly seen in these instructions, and through them there shines forth the Master's desire for fellowship with the guest; and all such fellowship must begin "in the lowest room," for that is the throne room of the Master.

There could be no embarrassment to the guest in the lowest room. He had been invited and was entitled to a place; and if by taking the lowest he was mistaken, the correction of the mistake could only mean "worship in the presence of them that sit at meat."

This advice of the Master points the way, the only way, to permanent and enjoyable exaltation—that which is given by the "Lord of all"—and that exaltation is given only to the meek in spirit.

Note the pattern of the Master's life, and His instruction to the invited guest will find its proper place.

The Father called upon His Son to be a guest of the human race. It was a long journey from the home of His preincarnate glory to the arms of a virgin girl. Whatever may have been His attributes before, of this we are sure: He had no "omni" qualities while on earth. He was not omnipresent, omnipotent, or omniscient while in the form of man; at least that is what He said.

If He had but descended from heavenly glory to the highest level of human existence, the step would have been well nigh infinite; but "being found in fashion as a man, he humbled himself" (Phil. 2:8) to the low position of servant, and lower still, He drank the cup of being made sin.

In His ministry, He claimed poverty and denied that He was One to sit at meat, but was among men as a servant. When returning from the field of toil, He prepared the meal for the household; and when they had eaten, He partook of what was left. He washed the dishes and the feet, and no one sat beneath Him; He had the lowest seat.

He did not thus sit in despondency, but in dignity and in faith. The laws of the Kingdom that He set forth for others to follow He knew full well would work for himself. He desired exaltation and even prayed, "O Father, glorify thou me" (John 17:5); but He despised self-exaltation and preached that "whosoever shall exalt himself shall be abased" (Matt 23:12). In the same breath, He extolled the exaltation of Another and pointed the way—the only way—to its attainment: "He that shall humble himself shall be exalted."

The closing chapter of His biography substantiated His claim. His exaltation grew out of His self-abasement. The "wherefore" of Phil. 2:9 is significant. The seat at the Father's right hand was given to Him because He had humbled himself.

What an exaltation it was! There was "given him a name which is above every name," "angels and authorities and powers being made subject unto him" (1 Pet. 3:22).

This high honor was not self-assumed; it was bestowed. He sat on the lowest seat, and the Lord of all escorted Him to the highest seat. "Christ glorified not himself . . . but he that said unto him, Thou art my son" (Heb. 5:5).

In His instruction to the "guest," He was exhorting us all to obey the law of the Kingdom and to rest assured that the trek downward led upward at last, not by self-seeking and human striving, but by a divine decree. The ascent is guaranteed by the descent.

In following the advice of the Master, fellowship is assured all the way. We begin with Him at the bottom and rise with Him to the heavenlies. "If we suffer, we shall also reign with him" (2 Tim. 2:12).

It takes faith to follow the Master—faith to believe that what He says is true, and faith to wait for its fulfillment. "The joy that was set before him" was distant, while the Cross "endured" was present (Heb. 12:2). The gap of time between promise and fulfillment must be spanned by the bridge of faith. The "lowest room" may be life's sole abode. While the higher one is "reserved in heaven for you" (1 Pet. 1:4), often the labors are in time and the reward in eternity. This led the great apostle to exclaim, "If in this life only we have hope in Christ, we are of all men most miserable" (1 Cor. 15:19).

Some receive partial payment in this life, as Daniel and the three Hebrew children, and others "died in faith, not having received the promises, but having seen them afar off" (Heb. 11:13).

Needless to say, the way pointed out by Jesus by example and by word is not the course recommended and followed by those of this world order. It was to correct the honor-seeking spirit of the "guests" that Jesus uttered His message. He was pointing the way to an enduring honor bestowed by the Master of the house.

In like manner, He is pointing us to an everlasting award, bestowed amid the splendor of the ages unending. He desires for all the highest and the best; and by His own blood drops, He marks the path to their attainment. Without the pattern of

His life we might falter by the way, but heeding the ex-hortation to "consider him . . . lest ye be wearied and faint in your minds" (Heb. 12:3), we press on, "being confident . . . that he which hath begun a good work in you will perform it until the day of Jesus Christ" (Phil. 1:6).

I Am Going to Hurt You

Many times I have heard kindhearted people say, "I wouldn't hurt you for anything." This sentiment sounds good; it is very soothing and satisfying. But let me tell you what I say: "I am going to hurt you. I will do it knowingly. You need to be hurt. To love is to hurt; hurting and healing cannot be divorced. To be healed, you must be hurt at times."

Before you conclude that you disagree with me, permit me to explain that to hurt is not the final result desired. To heal is the end to be reached, but the healing must often be preceded by the hurting; and since I am seeking to heal, I must not shun the hurting.

There are those who seem to believe that the healing process can be carried on without the hurting; but if they have found the painless path to health, they have found a way that I have not found, and have discovered a path unknown to God. If their painless method works, I would advise them to get in touch with the Almighty and bring Him in line with this up-to-date technique. I have been hearing that He is a little out-of-date; not modern in method; in fact, so set in His ways that He will not change! But I firmly believe that if He could be convinced of error, He would change, and it would be a feather in anyone's cap to know that he had properly instructed the Almighty and effected a needed reform. If and when this is done, I shall change my thesis from "I am going to hurt you" to "I wouldn't hurt you for anything"; but until then, "I mean to hurt you."

Actions must be judged by motive and results. The motive behind the hurting that I plan for you is love, and the result is spiritual growth and peace. Although my motive is love, and the end aimed at is growth, that end may not be reached, for the end reached by you does not depend upon my motive but upon your reaction.

There *are* hurts that are evilly motivated; the desired end is the hurt and not the healing. However, just as the hurt motivated by love and for a good purpose may not reach the desired end because the recipient takes a wrong attitude toward it, so in like manner, a sinfully motivated hurt intended to end in hurt can have its desired end of injury thwarted by the attitude of the one being injured. Following this principle, God is able to make the wrath of man to praise Him. It inspired Joseph to say to his wicked brethren,"Ye thought evil against me; but God meant it unto good" (Gen. 50:20).

Now let us view this matter in the light of God's Word. It reads, "Whom the Lord loveth he chasteneth" (Heb. 12:6). It further states, "Now no chastening for the present seemeth to be joyous, but grievous" (v. 11). The Word also states that He chastens us "for our profit, that we might be partakers of his holiness" (v. 10).

Here we have the whole process spelled out in clear terms. The motive of the chastening is love; the intermediate consequence is "grievous." The ultimate end in the mind of God is holiness.

Note, too, that the end that God has in mind may not be reached. It is reachable, for He never aims at anything that He cannot hit if not hindered by the one He desires to help. To obtain the helpful end (growth and soul peace), the one thus "loved" must be "exercised thereby" (v. 11). The key to success is in the hands of the one needing the healing.

It is evident that all whom God thus loves by chastening are not "exercised thereby." The record is "whom the Lord loveth he chasteneth, and scourgeth every son whom he receiveth." If all were "exercised thereby," they would all obtain

54

the "peaceable fruit of righteousness"; but some "fall away." The final result is determined by the one to whom God is seeking to impart holiness.

Now to look at my role as a servant, called of God to reconcile men to God; my duty here is clear—"reprove, rebuke, exhort with all longsuffering and doctrine" (2 Tim. 4:2). "Rebuke them sharply" (Titus 1:13); "exhort, and rebuke with all authority" (2:15). The motivation behind all of this must be love—love that will suffer in order to redeem, love that gives, love that will lay down its life for the brethren (see 1 John 3:16).

Here we are warned of possible failure: "For the time will come when they will not endure sound doctrine; . . . and they shall turn away their ears from the truth" (2 Tim. 4:3-4). In the light of this, Paul exhorts young Timothy to "watch . . . endure afflictions . . . make full proof of thy ministry" (v. 5).

The love that will rebuke must be strong, for at times it produces "afflictions" for the one thus loving. Paul met this and he wrote, "And I will very gladly spend and be spent for you; though the more abundantly I love you, the less I be loved" (2 Cor. 12:15).

The greatest Lover of them all was the most despised and rejected. To be like Him I, too, must bear a cross, the suffering of love unrequited; but the love of those who return love with love even unto death makes it worthwhile. Paul knew something of this experience too; to the Galatians he wrote, "Ye would have plucked out your own eyes, and have given them to me" (Gal. 4:15).

For more than half a century I have sought to serve God. I have needed reproof many times. That I know, for God has rebuked me often. My brethren have known it also. I have heard what they have said to others, but according to my present recollection, no one has ever rebuked me, or if they did, it was so mild that I cannot remember it. If at all, it was not "sharply."

The love that rebukes is very scarce. The reason? The would-be rebuker recoils from the suffering that might come upon himself; but Paul said to "endure afflictions" for "hereunto were ye called" (1 Pet. 2:21).

In the light of the "love" that I needed but did not get, I plan to love those to whom I minister. With the light that I have, I cannot do less and be a "good soldier." My love shall not be selfish, my hands unscarred, my heart unbroken. Love suffers. I shall love.

The Holy Spirit Needed Guidance

The Holy Spirit is a Guide, the divinely appointed Guide: 'He will guide you into all truth," said Jesus (John 16:13).

His leadership in our lives is proof of our sonship: "For as many as are led by the Spirit of God, they are the sons of God" (Rom. 8:14).

Could it be that the heavenly Guide must himself be guided? Yes, and why should that seem so strange when the only begotten Son of God needed to be guided? Said He, "I speak . . . those things which I have heard of [My Father]" (John 8:26), and it was said that Jesus was "led up of the Spirit into the wilderness to be tempted" (Matt. 4:1). He was not guided by the voice of His own being, but by the voice of His Father from above, and the Holy Spirit was guided by the Father.

Of this speaking Spirit who was sent to lead us, it was said, "He shall not speak of himself; but whatsoever he shall hear, that shall he speak" (John 16:13). He was first a student and then a teacher, a listener and then a speaker.

What practical lessons may we learn from our great Teacher? Surely we should know that if He needed to listen to God, how much more we need to listen! It should be remembered that it is said, "They shall be all taught of God" (John 6:45). We have the same Teacher as Christ had. How foolish it is for us to "lean [to our] own understanding" (Prov. 3:5) when neither Jesus nor the Holy Spirit would do so.

From this and other similar facts we should know that God the Father is the final word in His universe, and the Spirit and the Son sought out His will and obeyed it.

Note the progressiveness in the Spirit's hearing: "whatsoever he shall hear," not whatsoever He had heard (past tense), but whatsoever He was hearing. This too follows the pattern of the Son, who received His instructions as He went along. The "will shew" of John 5:20 gives us insight into the progressiveness of the Father's revelations to His Son.

Paul tells us that the Holy Spirit "searcheth all things, yea, the deep things of God" (1 Cor. 2:10). He is an explorer and a revealer of truth to those who desire to explore.

The faithfulness of the Spirit's ministry is clearly implied: "Whatsoever he shall hear, that shall he speak." This too follows the pattern of the Son who said, "I speak to the world those things which I have heard of him" (John 8:26), and again, "I have given unto them the words which thou gavest me" (17:8).

The words of Jesus were at times disturbing and hard to bear. He called people "liars," "whited sepulchres," "hypocrites," "blind leaders of the blind," "murderers," "adulterers," and even more (e.g., Matt 23:13-39).

He was a true prophet and was true to His message. He was not afraid of what man could do to Him. They did their worst and He survived, and He tells us to follow Him without fear.

The Holy Spirit's ministry was disturbing also. When Peter preached at Pentecost under the power of the Holy Spirit, the hearts of the people were "pricked." The Holy Spirit was pricking Saul on the way to Damascus; and when He can have His free course in the hearts of His messengers, their message (or His through them) will prick too.

It is safe to abandon oneself to the leadership of the Holy

Spirit, for He has been instructed what to say and what to do, and His orders have come from the throne of the Almighty.

This insight into the ministry of both the Son and the Holy Spirit but points up Paul's statement, "But to us there is but one God, the Father" (1 Cor. 8:6). His Representatives upon earth—the Son and the Holy Spirit—sat at His feet and took orders from Him and carried out His will perfectly.

Against this background of the utter dependence of the Son and the Holy Spirit upon the Father, we should view our lack of dependence and our neglect of His school. The whole world would instantly change if all men could, or rather would, recognize their utter dependence upon God. That will not be in our world order, but it is our desire to see as many as possible thus changed, for only the one that does the will of the Father "abideth for ever" (1 John 2:17).

The Holy Spirit listens—could it be? What a thought! Was it necessary? The answer must be yes. And the reason? There can be no oneness outside the Father. He is the Head, and all others must conform to the Head.

If both the Son and the Holy Spirit listen to and are guided by the Father, can anything but absolute obedience make us, His children, eligible to live with Him? The answer is, obedience to Him must be full and complete, or we cannot live with Him. Jesus and the Holy Spirit have come to show us the way and the potential cost of following in their path.

It is the desire of the Holy Spirit to flow through our lives without hindrance. Too often, at best, the flow is a trickle, when He has pictured it as a "well of water springing up" or as "rivers of living water" flowing out (John 4:14; 7:38).

Our lives are not to be stagnant pools, or wells to be drawn from, but outflowing streams. Why is a spring a spring? Because it is connected with a source higher than itself. Jesus could announce that He was the Water of Life because He was connected with a Source higher than himself—"My Father is greater than I" (John 14:28), and from that "greater" there flowed from the Son living water. His children are supposed to be of that pattern, pouring out "rivers" of living water. Soul searching should be in order and Christlikeness sought.

The Speaking Spirit

"God, who at sundry times and in divers manners spake in time past unto the fathers by the prophets, hath in these last days spoken unto us by his Son" (Heb. 1:1-2).

The inspired Word, "God, who at sundry times and in divers manners spake in time past unto the fathers by the prophets," introduces us to an established method of God's revelations to men. The records of the ancient inspired writers verify the accuracy of this statement—God did speak in "divers manners" and at many "sundry times" to the fathers.

Numerous, and at times strange, were the methods that He employed to bring His message to men. Sometimes He appeared to them in dreams in the night, sometimes in strange and almost grotesque visions, one time through the speech of the humble donkey, at times by white-winged angels, laddering their way between earth and heaven; at times He manifested himself by heavenly messengers in the form of neighborly men, at times by cloud-borne horses and horsemen, at times by the movement of the elements—raging winds, falling fire, or violent earthquake; and at other times by a gentle whispering voice.

Whatever the method divinely employed, God was able to get His message to His prophets, and through them to others. Not only were the manners of revelation very diverse, but also the times of the revelations were "sundry." No fixed pattern of time or place can be traced. He came to some while they were feeding their flocks in the open field; to others as they lay upon their beds; to another as he was gathering fruit; to another in the prison cell; to another in a king's lavish court; to yet another while in forced exile from home and native land.

He spoke to the captain as he entered the battle; He spoke of victory when apparent disaster seemed inevitable; He spoke of famine; He spoke in the Tabernacle when insurrection arose; He spoke in the Temple when invasion was near. He spoke when the flag of triumph perched upon the staffs of their victorious armies, and when they bowed their heads to the invading enemy. He spoke to youth in the house of God, and to the infirm upon his couch of pain. He spoke when sin had engulfed the soul of a noble king, and when the sun-scorched earth was to receive its refreshing rain. Yes, God spoke again and again at "sundry times" and in "divers manners," and His message was clear and understandable both as to its nature and its Author: God spoke and men understood, and knew that it was God speaking.

For centuries the Israelites believed that God had spoken to their fathers. This they seemed never to doubt. Then came the clearer and more advanced method of the divine speaking: "God . . . hath in these last days spoken unto us by his Son."

Although Christ's contemporaries affirmed, "We know that God spake unto Moses" (John 9:29), nevertheless they refused to listen to or believe the message spoken by His only begotten Son. How strange does this appear! The same Speaker—the Almighty—but a different representative, and no response! How could this be?

The answer seems clear, elucidated by statements made by the Speaker himself. Their claims of faith in what Moses said were empty claims. They mouthed words that they did not believe. They had a form of belief, but it was void of life-giving power. Jesus challenged the validity of their professed faith in the divineness of Moses' message. Said He, "For had ye believed Moses, ye would have believed me: for he wrote of me" (John 5:46).

The Jews of Jesus' day had faith in a speaking God of the yesterdays, but who, for all practical purposes, was dead. They gloried in a belief in a God that was alive and speaking in the distant day of Moses and the prophets, but denied that He was longer speaking. Their faith was in the dead letter and not in the still-living Speaker.

Notwithstanding the reaction of the unbelieving Jews to the divine message of His Son, God was speaking nonetheless to them and to all ages following. What a message it was! "Never man spake like this man" (John 7:46) was the united voice of some of their most brilliant lawyers. Christ spake as one having authority, and not as the scribes—that they were willing to admit and never deny. They had their own reasons for denying the divinity of His message, but they could not deny its power to move the minds of men. God was speaking through His only begotten Son. His message was to transcend all the messages of the past and was to endure for all time.

The messages came in many forms, on many occasions, and to widely varied groups. He spoke to the throngs by the wayside, the multitudes that followed Him to the desert place. He addressed the annual worshipers at the Temple and those who assembled in the synagogues on the Sabbath days. He taught by the seaside, in the homes of the rich and the poor alike. He ministered in the humble home of His three friends at Bethany and sat teaching at the festive board of a notorious sinner. He graced weddings with His ministry and visited the famous pool of Bethesda with His message of healing.

He spoke in parables to all that had ears to hear. He directed His message of repentance and divine forgiveness to all, and deeper messages to those who had begun their journey with Him. He spoke! He spoke boldly and yet with compassion. He marked the way to heaven in all necessary detail. The path He marked was straight. No one need stumble in the taking, for He promised the light of His own presence to all who would enter the heavenly way.

He spoke loudly and clearly in understandable words, but the miracle of His acts spoke more loudly than did His words. He appealed on one occasion for what He said to what He did, and challenged the listeners to believe on Him for what they saw Him do, if what He said was not to them convincing.

He spoke, and His message was the message of God. It was delivered openly and without fear. The common people listened to it, and so did the rulers of the Jews. They did not heed, but they heard. He spoke, and all could hear who would.

Many heard His message and in time believed. The century of which He was a part heard Him in a marked way. Upon His resurrection, thousands and hundreds of thousands heeded His message and became His ardent followers.

In the opening centuries of the Christian era the faith in a speaking God was strong, and in Christendom today there is a universal belief that God did speak to us by Jesus Christ. Every Christian, properly so called, will affirm that belief today.

Nevertheless, there has developed a widespread belief that God no longer speaks—that Christ was the last divine Spokesman.

As the Jews would give their lives for their belief that God spake by Moses and the prophets, but was no longer speaking in the day that His Son was upon earth, so there are many today who will fight furiously in proclaiming their faith that God did speak to us by His Son, and yet, as did the Jews of Jesus' day, they deny that God still speaks today.

Certainly we are not claiming that a new Bible should be

written nor that the one that we have should be amended. It contains all that we need to point us to a Savior, and therein is direction enough to guide us safely from earth to heaven. We firmly believe all that Jesus said, and we believe it is full and final. It is because we do believe that He was speaking the message of God that we come with this emphasis—an emphasis given by Jesus himself. If it were not from Him, we might well pass it by, but the message is from Him.

What is His message at this point? John, for one, states it, using Jesus' own words:

"But the Comforter, which is the Holy Ghost, whom the Father will send in my name, he shall teach you all things, and bring all things to your remembrance, whatsoever I have said unto you. . . .

"He will guide you into all truth: for he shall not speak of himself; but whatsoever he shall hear, that shall he speak: and he will shew you things to come.

"He shall glorify me: for he shall receive of mine, and shall shew it unto you" (John 14:26; 16:13-14).

Here the speaking Christ tells us plainly that heavenly speaking is not over. Some, like the Jews of Christ's day who clung to the speaking God of Moses' day but denied the speaking Son, may now be clinging dogmatically and fanatically to the belief that God spoke by His Son, but at the same time vigorously denying what the Son said—namely, the Holy Spirit would be a Speaker, a Teacher, and a Revealer of things to come. This would be much stranger than it is were it not for the fact that the very same thing was done in the days of Christ—not by the illiterate rabble but by the religious leaders of the day. The top teachers of the Word of God—those who "sat in Moses' seat"—denied that there would be a speaking Son, although Jesus said that Moses wrote of Him.

In many circles of religion, the speaking Spirit is unheeded and even denied by those who feverishly defend a dead faith in a once-speaking Son.

When the Old Testament prophets wanted to contrast Jehovah with idols, they referred to the idols as having eyes, but they could not see; they had ears, but they could not hear; they had feet, but they could not walk. This was but a graphic way of saying that the living God is a seeing, speaking, mobile God.

Our religion is a religion of a Christ who once spoke and is still speaking through the Holy Spirit, whom He sent upon His followers at Pentecost, and announced that He is available to all of His believing followers even until the end of the age.

The Spirit can speak as clearly, as understandably, to the soul of man today as God spoke to Moses and the prophets, and as clearly as He spoke to the world through Jesus Christ. But it is unreasonable to think that He can get His message through to the soul that has been galvanized against the truth of the Master's word concerning the Spirit's speaking.

God has not grown dumb just because He wrote a Book. God is the same yesterday, today, and forever, and still speaks in understandable soul language to those who have ears to hear. This is a central part of the Son's message: "Hear ye him."

We Cannot Deny It

The words of my theme strike into a very tender spot of my soul. They have challenged me for over half a century; and when I have considered them seriously and honestly, they have troubled me greatly.

To understand the problem, one needs to see it in the light of its setting. Jesus Christ had just finished His three years of disturbing ministry. The religionists of His day had been challenged and found to be wanting in spiritual power, and void of sincerity. He had challenged their honesty and called them hypocrites. Their hypocrisy had been laid bare before the whole world, and in anger they had rid themselves of Him, so they thought. The remaining task was to clear the field of His influence and to destroy the influence and, if need be, the lives of His followers. Their position in the religious world was at stake. If the influence of the Nazarene were to continue in force, their thrones would tumble; therefore, there must be an end to all of His teachings and His teachers.

The sharp arrow of the Galilean's messages had been reinforced and driven home by the miraculous deeds that He performed. It left them without defense. He had said, "If I had not done among them the works which none other man did, they had not had sin" (John 15:24). Thus speaking, He was placing His deeds above His words as instruments of effective witnessing. On another occasion He had emphasized this truth: "Though ye believe not me, believe the works: that ye may know" (10:38). He had affirmed that the miraculous works that He did established His claims of being sent by the Father. He affirmed, "The works that I do in my Father's name, they bear witness of me" (v. 25).

Since the power of His life was in His God-wrought deeds, if His power and influence were to be stopped, He must be silenced. This they did. No longer would there be men born blind who were now walking their city streets with full vision. The Healer being silenced, they could build up their charge that He had been doing His mighty deeds by the power of Beelzebub. They knew that He had a few ardent followers, but with the miracle-working power of His life removed, the strength of the movement would be sapped, and His cause would soon perish. This must have been their thinking, so it was to their advantage to crush everything that looked like an act of God. They would use every means, fair or foul, to accomplish this.

There had been quite a demonstration on the day of Pentecost, but most of that could be well accounted for as extreme emotionalism and a flare of dedication to a martyred leader. It would soon subside or be easily crushed.

To their amazement, however, something happened that they could not cope with. The supernatural had taken place, and it was in support of the cause that had been sponsored by the Crucified. In fact, it was ascribed to the power and presence of the One that they had put to death. This was damaging evidence against them. What could they do?

The undeniable facts were examined. A lame man had been healed. If he had been a citizen of a remote community and known only to a few, the problem would not have been so serious, but he was a mature man who was known to the whole worshiping community. His prominent place at the Temple gate made his condition known to all, and his leaping and praising God in the Temple before all the people placed thousands on the witness stand in favor of the healers.

The onlookers "were filled with wonder and amazement" (Acts 3:10). The disciples were not amazed. They had expected such things. Jesus had promised them that they could perform such miraculous feats in His name. Peter, the spokesman, "answered unto the people, Ye men of Israel, why marvel ye at this?" (v. 12). It was no marvel to him. He expected such things.

To add to the seriousness of the matter for the Jews, Peter ascribed the power for this great work to the Christ whom they had crucified. The fat was in the fire! The fact could not be denied. The miraculous had not ceased with the death of the Master. The sin and the guilt of the Crucifixion was laid at the feet of the Jews, and the charge backed up by an act of divine power. The evidence was so clear and indisputable that His most bitter enemies affirmed, "We cannot deny it" (4:16). They *wanted* to deny it. They would have given much for that ability, but the facts that they themselves knew were beyond denial, and the tide of public sentiment made a denial dangerous and futile.

Such was the nature of the healings of the early Christian era. The friends of the disciples believed them fully, as did the multitude, and the enemies openly admitted that they were beyond dispute.

I know of no miracle of the New Testament that was so anemic that it was denied. Only one do I recall bore the element of the delayed or gradual healing. With this possible exception, they were thrilling and awe-inspiring. What God was doing in healings was not to be confused by the work of physicians; but when they were mentioned together, it was in contrast. The woman who had spent all that she had with doctors and "was nothing better" found instant healing with the Master. Such were the God-revealing miracles in the days of Christ and His disciples.

How different it is today! Many say it is supposed to be different, that the day of the miracle is past, and that is in the plan of God. Without debating that point, I do affirm that such days have passed, in the main at least. I am not a skeptic. I believe that God's power has not diminished, and I do not believe that His plan to heal has changed. The change has been in His professed followers. And as I am not a skeptic, neither am I a liar. I will not claim to believe what I do not believe in. I can speak only from my viewpoint, but when speaking, I will be honest.

I wish I had been in that company that day who said, "We cannot deny it"—it is a God-wrought miracle! We cannot deny it! I can honestly affirm that in a lifetime I have never seen anything wrought in the texture of man's body that I could affirm, without reasonable doubt, that God did. I wish that this were not true, but God knows that I speak the truth. What you may have seen does not change my testimony. I just haven't seen it.

I am near my 70th year in the ministry. I have preached in nearly all of the states of the Union and have spoken in hundreds of different churches. I have attended hundreds of healing services and have participated in many of them. I have seen thousands of people anointed for healing and have heard many testimonies. Many cases I have followed up to see the final and permanent results, if any. I have seen nothing that I could not honestly deny as being divine. I long to see something in this field that I can honestly ascribe to God. Thus far I have not found it.

I have been close enough to the populace to hear the underbreath remarks of those that attend such healing services, and they have been unconvinced. In all the cases that I have witnessed, the crutches that bore the would-be healed to the altar bore him away, and the chair that was used to bring the patient was used to roll him around later. I find little, if any, difference in the recovery of the two men in the same hospital, operated on the same day by the same doctor for the same malady, when one was a Nazarene pastor and the other a cursing bartender. There is, as E. Stanley Jones points out, a margin of favor to the Christian because of his good living and spirit of courage, but this is beside the point at issue.

Speaking generally, we know that God is the Giver of all strength that is used in recovery. One could not curse or commit adultery without strength that God alone can give. Such strength comes to all through the overall plan of God in His creative act. We should praise God for such strength that He has given to all of His creatures. In the case of the normal recovery, or even a little better than normal recovery, of the Christian that is prayed for, thanksgiving should be given to God for such universal provision and not to man's faith for healing. This would leave the field open for the more specific work of God that we are discussing as the miraculous.

This whole thesis thus far is only background for a question. The question is, Why the well-nigh sterile condition of our healing ministry? This is a timely question, and it comes as an honest challenge to the status quo. Is this the normal way, or have we missed the mark? Has God changed? Has He reversed His practice? Is He pleased with the way in which we are going? Will we honestly face this issue? Though we can't be all-wise, we can be honest, if we will.

And So It Came to Pass

"This was the word of the Lord which he spake unto Jehu, saying, Thy sons shall sit on the throne of Israel unto the fourth generation. And so it came to pass" (2 Kings 15:12).

Because Jehu, king of Israel, had executed the judgment of God against the house of wicked Ahab and had "destroyed Baal out of Israel," the Lord made him the promise of the text.

In fulfillment of that promise, his son, grandson, great-grandson, and finally his great-great-grandson occupied the throne of Israel. (See 2 Kings 10:30.)

The important thing about this story is not that five kings of the same family had occupied the throne of Israel in unbroken succession, but that the event was told in advance—even before the first of the five had left the throne. "And so it came to pass" could be spoken reliably only by the One who could say to Jeremiah, "Before I formed thee in the belly I knew thee; and before thou camest forth out of the womb I sanctified thee, and I ordained thee a prophet unto the nations" (Jer. 1:5). The Lord is the One, and the only One, who could name unborn sons and, in the midst of national conflict and political feuds, keep four generations of them alive until each of them would fulfill His promise. Herein lies the importance of the promise.

This story underlines two very important facts:

First: God is a speaking God. The record is, "This was the word of the Lord which he spake unto Jehu."

Second: God proves himself in His ability to foretell the future. "Thy children of the fourth generation shall sit on the throne of Israel" (2 Kings 10:30).

Jesus, following the same pattern, said to His disciples, "Now I tell you before it come, that, when it is come to pass, ye may believe that I am he" (John 13:19).

It seems that God has been very anxious to keep these two truths alive in the thinking and hearts of His followers. We have been warned, "Take heed, brethren, lest there be in any of you an evil heart of unbelief, in departing from the living God" (Heb. 3:12). The Holy Spirit has been given to us that we may know "things to come," for that is one of the assignments of the Holy Spirit (John 16:13).

It seems that there is a desperate need of a revival of these two great truths. It is so easy to become so enthusiastic about the historic Christ that we settle for a cold, intellectual belief in Him, without knowing anything of a living, speaking Christ.

This was the way of the religionists of Christ's day. The leaders of the Jews would sacrifice their lives on the fact that God was a speaking God in the days of Moses, but they denied His voice when He was speaking through His Son. They had a dead belief in an ancient God, but no living faith in One who could speak currently.

The "living God" stands at the center of the Christian's life. If alive, then He can reveal himself to us. Nothing short of this is true religion. Otherwise it is but an empty form—a "form of godliness" from which all life has gone (2 Tim. 3:5).

The strength of the Christian life is this self-revealing, living God. The final assurance of one's salvation is based upon this revelation to us: "The Spirit itself beareth witness with our spirit, that we are the children of God" (Rom. 8:16).

We dare not rest our souls on any other foundation. This

is the basic proof that He is alive. Knowing His voice here, it is less difficult to understand His voice at other times.

The second great fact—the fact that God alone can foretell events accurately—is illustrated in the text. Although this illustration is taken from the history of an ancient people, it is up-to-date. The Holy Spirit has been designated to carry on this foretelling. When the Spirit reveals to one of the Lord's followers something of the future, and in due time it comes to pass, this strengthens the faith of the saint in the living God.

Since this ministry of the Spirit's foretelling events to the saints is such a great stimulation to faith, the enemy is ever on the alert to destroy this means of spiritual edification. One of the most prolific and successful means that he uses to annul this work of the Spirit is to mimic the Holy Spirit's voice and deceive immature Christians, thus discrediting this most important phase of God's plan for the strengthening of His children and the advancement of His kingdom. Because of so much counterfeit abroad, some well-meaning Christians— even ministers of the gospel—have discouraged those who would thus know this ministry of the Holy Spirit.

There should be a revival of Christian understanding and experience with the speaking God and the foretelling Spirit.

I Am Expecting Angels

(Heb. 1:14)

Perhaps we do not make as much of angels as we should. We live in a materialistic age, and little thought is given to the invisible, the spiritual, and the spirits.

For guidance here, we must turn to the only authentic guidebook there is—the Word of God. The duties of angels are clearly stated thus: "Are they not all ministering spirits, sent forth to minister for them who shall be heirs of salvation?" (Heb. 1:14). In another clear passage, we have, "The angel of the Lord encampeth round about them that fear him, and delivereth them" (Ps. 34:7).

It would appear from at least two passages in the Word that an angel or angels are assigned to people and persons. In Dan. 12:1, we read, "And at that time shall Michael stand up, the great prince which standeth for the children of thy people."

When Rhoda went to the door and found Peter and reported it to the prayers, they couldn't believe it and said, "It is his angel" (Acts 12:15).

When Jesus was blessing little children, He said, "That in heaven their angels do always behold the face of my Father which is in heaven" (Matt. 18:10).

It would appear that each child had a guardian angel standing before the Father, ready for any orders of service assigned to them for the children. They are called "ministering spirits," and the title is meaningless if they never minister. It could be that many a danger has already been averted in our lives by the invisible hand of a protecting angel.

We know from both testaments something of the appearances and work of angels. They protected Elisha at Dothan. One stayed the hand of Abraham lest he kill his son. When Abraham sent his servant to seek a wife for Isaac, he told him that God would send an angel before him and prosper him. The events following give credence to the belief of Abraham.

Moses said that God "sent an angel, and hath brought us forth out of Egypt" (Num. 20:16).

It was an angel that brought to Manoah the announcement of a son.

An angel touched Elijah as he slept under a juniper tree and asked him to arise and eat the meal prepared for him.

"And God sent an angel unto Jerusalem to destroy it" (1 Chron. 21:15).

God sent an angel to protect the three Hebrew children and to deliver Daniel from the den of lions.

It was an angel who announced the coming of both Christ and John the Baptist, His forerunner.

It was an angel who opened the door to Cornelius' house and directed him to a gospel minister.

An angel advised Peter to bind on his sandals and get ready for an escape. He then opened the gates and sent the free prisoner on his way to liberty.

The New Testament is replete with stories of angelic ministrations. They opened prison doors, directed evangelists in their ministry, told of coming events, and otherwise assisted in Kingdom work. They were not always visible, but it seems that they were ever present.

The closing days of human history, as told in advance and recorded in the Book of Revelation, are filled with the activities of angels. They have been active in the past and will be in the future, but what about the present? Has their ministry been canceled? Why do so few, if any, appear?

This raises some serious thoughts—thoughts that we may well ponder with deep honesty. Look at the record and see when angels did appear—to whom? under what conditions? and for what purpose?

Given a casual glance at angelic activity, it will be noted that they came to back up men who were in desperate straits in the service of God—men who were fighting the battles of the Lord and counting not their own lives dear unto themselves. Check the list and note the facts.

There was Moses, who had forsaken a royal crown to follow the call of God. There were Daniel and the three Hebrew children, who chose rather to die than betray their Lord. There was Elijah, and other messengers of God who had joined the ranks of the prophets of whom Stephen said, "Which of the prophets have not your fathers persecuted?" (Acts 7:52). And Jesus lamented, "O Jerusalem . . . which killest the prophets, and stonest them that are sent unto thee" (Luke 13:34).

There was Paul, who had suffered the loss of all things for Christ; and Peter, who dared the Jewish council and in bold defiance said, "Whether it be right in the sight of God to hearken unto you more than unto God, judge ye" (Acts 4:19), and they went out to preach in obedience to Christ and in defiance of the mandates of men. Then came the stripes, the jail, the angel, the extension of the Kingdom.

Are angels resting because there is no worthwhile Christian enterprises worthy of their help? Is there no one going to the lions' den in defense of his faith, that causes God to order angelic assistance? Is there no one exhausted in Gethsemane's conflict who can only be revived by the ministry of angels?

Do we need angelic help for what we are doing? Isn't the assumed task man-size, and no heavenly aid needed?

Just where are the angels, and why don't they come? Have we watered down our message by our itching ears? Are we seeking to please men rather than God? Are we willing to suffer, and do we follow Him so closely that we will?

"Oh, come, angel bands, around me stand." I go the way with Him, where you will be needed. I am expecting angels. They have been promised.